A Day in the Life of a Veterinarian

A Day in the Life

# of a Veterinarian

WILLIAM
JASPERSOHN

LITTLE, BROWN AND COMPANY   BOSTON   TORONTO

FIRST EDITION

T09/78

Library of Congress Cataloging in Publication Data

Jaspersohn, William.
   A day in the life of a veterinarian.

   SUMMARY: Follows a veterinarian as he treats
patients in his clinic and operating rooms, makes farm
visits, and takes emergency calls.
    1. Veterinary medicine—Juvenile literature.
2. Sequist, David B. 3. Veterinarians—Vermont—
Juvenile literature. [1. Veterinary medicine.
2. Veterinarians] I. Title.
SF756.J37   636.089′092′4   78-13584
ISBN 0-316-45810-4

*Published simultaneously in Canada
by Little, Brown & Company (Canada) Limited*

PRINTED IN THE UNITED STATES OF AMERICA

For Pam,
who loves geese

I wish to express my gratitude to the following persons whose assistance to this book has been invaluable: Mrs. Rene Binginot, David Braun, Miss Barbara Chausse, Mrs. John Farmer, Mr. and Mrs. Richard Fifield, John Hall, Mr. and Mrs. Harry McCuen, Miss Ellen Menard, Miss Diane Merrill, Dr. Roger Murray, Dr. and Mrs. Hartley Neel, Dr. Gordon Nielson, William Small, Mrs. Polly Whitcomb, S. Francis Woods.

And to the following institutions: Department of Animal Pathology, University of Vermont; Department of Entomology, University Extension Service, University of Vermont; Discovery Museum, Essex Junction, Vermont; Vermont Department of Fish and Game.

I would also like to thank my brothers, Ron and Paul Jaspersohn; my grandmother-in-law, Louise R. Cunningham; my parents-in-law, Dr. and Mrs. Peter R. Cunningham; and my parents, Mr. and Mrs. Paul Jaspersohn, for their very special support.

I could not have finished this book without the timely help of my good friend Ward Rice, who printed the photographs, and whose advice and technical expertise were a blessing.

I am indebted to Dr. Alan Lindsey, Alan Morton, and Sue May, who were always helpful when I was working at the hospital.

Finally, I would like to thank Dr. Sequist and his family and all his wonderful animal patients for actually making this book possible.

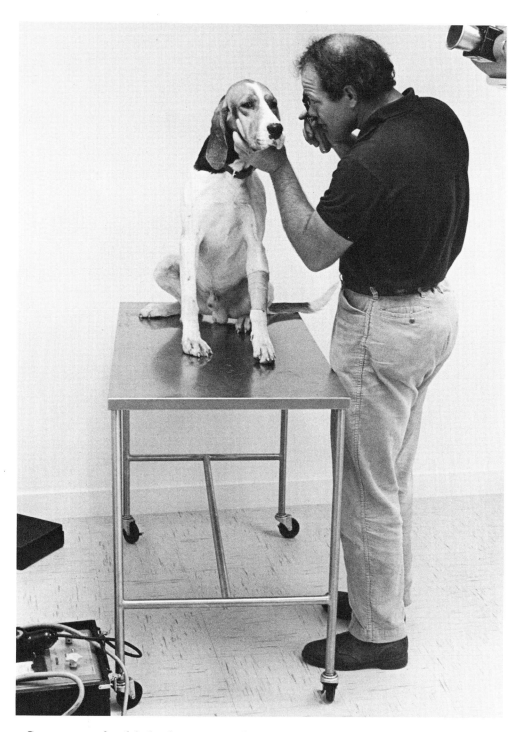

Some people think that a veterinarian only takes care of dogs and cats. But depending on where he lives, a veterinarian takes care of many other animals besides. A country veterinarian takes care of cows, for instance, and horses, sheep, pigs, goats, ducks, chickens, geese, parrots, parakeets, gerbils, hamsters, even raccoons and skunks sometimes. This veterinarian has taken care of them all. He lives in Vermont, and his name is Dr. David B. Sequist.

Dr. Sequist grew up in Connecticut. As a boy he worked on different farms. He majored in chemistry at the University of Vermont and played football on the varsity team. After graduation he went to Cornell University, where he studied at the New York State College of Veterinary Medicine. In his last year at Cornell, he married his wife, Jane.

The Sequists have three children. Their sons, Tom and Larsen, like swimming and fishing, and their daughter, Hannah, likes to ski. And all three Sequist children love animals. They have two dogs, two cats, a horse named Willow, and four baby calves, whose names are Betty, Boss, Lucy, and Jo.

Dr. Sequist is director of the Sequist Animal Hospital, which is located in Morrisville, Vermont. The building is new and modern. It has cages for small animals, such as dogs and cats, and stalls for big animals, such as horses and cows. It has a pharmacy for storing drugs, two examining rooms, two operating rooms, and an X-ray room. The other veterinarian at the Sequist Hospital, Dr. Alan Lindsey, also studied at Cornell. It takes at least two years of college and then four years of veterinary school to become a veterinarian. Then you have to pass a group of tests to get a state license. It isn't easy, but Dr. Sequist says that for anyone who loves to work with animals, it's worth it. He wouldn't trade jobs with anybody.

Every morning at eight o'clock, five days a week, Dr. Sequist arrives at the hospital for work. One thing he likes about his job is that because he works for himself, he can set his own hours. He can even wear whatever clothes he wants. On spring days like today, he likes wearing jeans and a knit shirt the best.

He tries to spend the first half hour of every morning paying the hospital's bills and balancing its books. Some mornings there isn't enough time, though.

Soon the rest of the staff starts arriving. Alan Morton cleans the cages. He is Dr. Sequist's assistant and has been with the hospital for six years. There's always cleaning up to do around the hospital because the doctor likes to keep things spotless.

There's always traveling to do, too. Farm animals are big, and farmers don't like to bring them to the hospital unless they're very sick and need operations. So the doctors visit the animals on the different farms. Sometimes between them, the two doctors travel two thousand miles in one week of visiting farm patients.

Today Dr. Lindsey will check on some sick cows. Dr. Sequist shows him the list.

Like any doctors, veterinarians carry kit bags, and Dr. Lindsey likes to make sure that his is full before starting on the road each morning. Then, while he packs his car, Dr. Sequist helps Alan hose down the big-animal room because a horse is coming in later today for X rays.

Nine o'clock. Now the receptionist, Sue May, arrives and starts taking appointments. You have to call a few days in advance to get an appointment at the hospital, unless you have an emergency. Then Sue will tell you to bring your pet in right away.

Dr. Sequist always checks over the day's appointment schedule with Sue before starting work. Then the real day begins.

Mornings at the hospital are usually divided into three parts: cage work, for animals with special problems; small-animal clinic, which is mostly for dogs and cats; and surgery, for any animals big or small.

The doctor never knows what to expect when he goes to the cage room because animals are often brought in before he arrives. One morning he might find a pig with a chest cold. Another morning a husky with a toothache might be waiting.

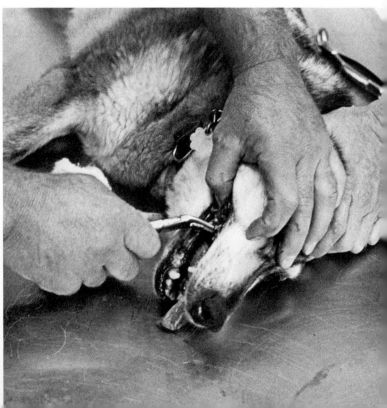

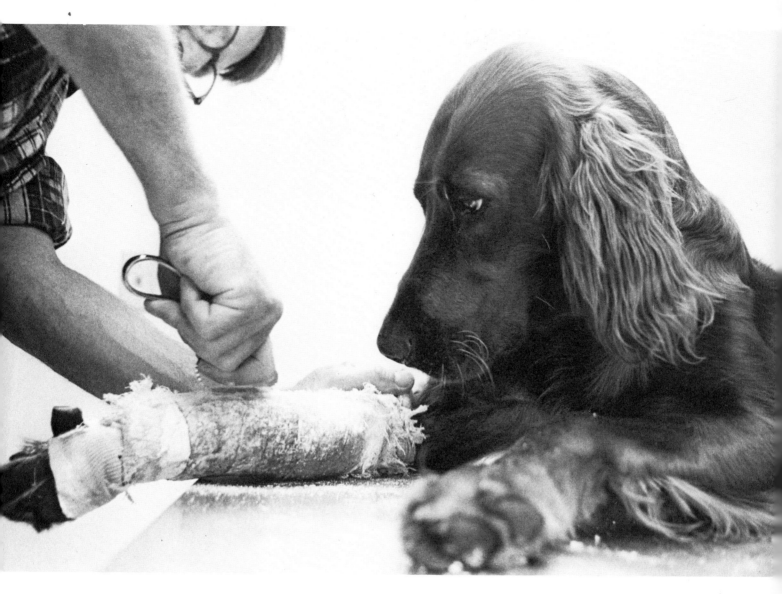

On this particular morning the doctor finds an old friend waiting for him, a red Irish setter named Plumley. Three weeks ago Plumley was hit by a car, and Dr. Sequist had to do emergency surgery on his broken leg. He took X rays and put a steel pin in the leg to hold the two pieces of broken bone together, and then sewed up the cut he had to make in Plumley's skin. He wrapped the leg in a plaster cast to keep it straight, and then gave Plumley shots to stop infections. The operation took two hours, but Plumley never felt anything. The doctor had given him a drug called an *anesthetic* to make him sleep while the operation took place.

Now, three weeks later, it's time to change the cast and take out the stitches. Alan Morton starts the procedure by cutting away the old cast with a sharp-toothed knife.

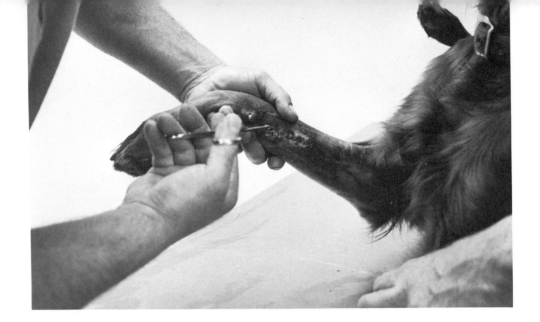

Dr. Sequist says that snipping out stitches is easy if you have the right scissors, but you still have to be careful. You don't want to stab the patient.

The pin connecting Plumley's broken leg is eight inches long and one-eighth of an inch thick. A little bit of the pin sticks out through the skin so that the doctor can pull it out later when the bone has healed. The pin has to stay in for three more weeks.

For now, though, Plumley seems content to have the stitches out.

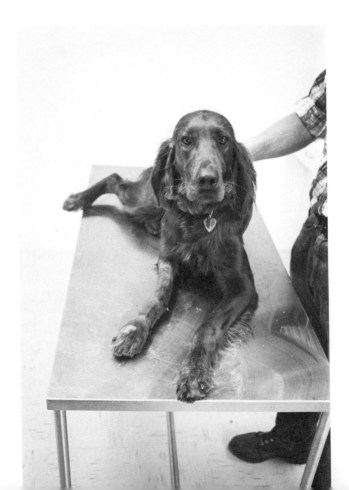

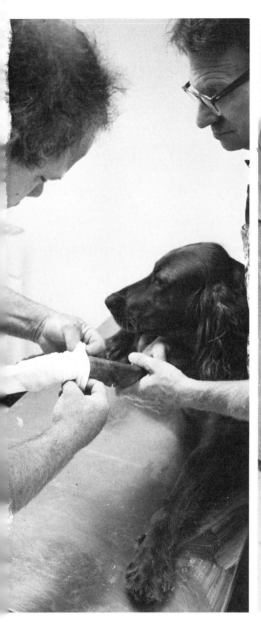
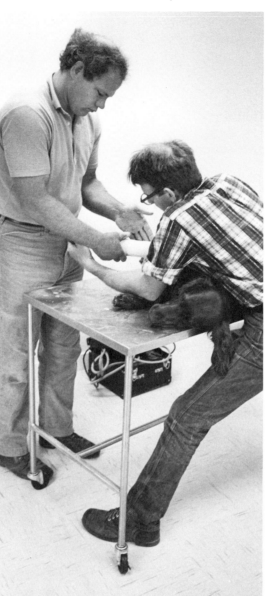

After snipping away the stitches, the doctor slides a fresh protective sleeve over Plumley's leg, then wraps everything in plaster bandage. Good veterinarians have to like to work with their hands, and Dr. Sequist likes working with his. His favorite part of putting on a cast is smoothing in the wet plaster. The whole secret of wrapping a cast, he says, is knowing how much pressure to apply.

Plumley will stay in a cage until his master comes to pick him up this afternoon. Dr. Sequist is pleased with the way the bone is knitting. He thinks that Plumley's leg will soon be as good as new.

By the time Dr. Sequist and Alan have finished with Plumley, the waiting room is filled with people and their pets all waiting for the start of small-animal clinic. Sometimes the waiting room can get noisy, especially when dogs *and* cats are waiting. Once in a while someone brings in a pet goat, and then it gets very noisy.

The doctor barely has time to wash his hands before seeing the first clinic patient, a kitten that has come for her rabies and distemper shots.

The kitten's name is Tinkerbell. Her owner is a girl named Jennifer, who wants to be with her pet but doesn't like shots.

Dr. Sequist knows this, but he also knows that he has to vaccinate Tinkerbell against distemper and rabies. He loads a hypodermic syringe with one cubic centimeter, or *c.c.*, of distemper vaccine, which he stores in a refrigerator until it's time to use it. Dr. Sequist gives about one thousand rabies and distemper shots a year, and he puts the needle in straight so that the patients hardly feel it. People always ask him if he practiced giving shots on oranges in veterinary school, but he didn't; he practiced on animals. Now he gives Tinkerbell her two shots under the skin, or *subcutaneously* as he would say.

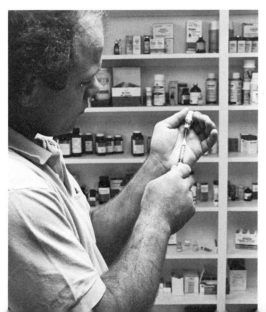
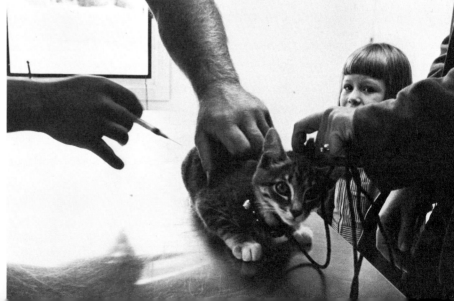

Tinkerbell is vaccinated and it didn't hurt a bit. She now will be safe from rabies for two and a half years and from distemper for one year. Then she'll have to come back for a new shot.

Vaccinations are important, says Dr. Sequist, because rabies and distemper are terrible diseases — rabies especially, because it can kill people. Infected animals spread rabies through their saliva, usually by biting unvaccinated animals. The rabies virus destroys brain cells, and the rabid animal first turns vicious, then becomes paralyzed, and finally dies. Distemper, which is a disease of the nerves, lungs, and digestive system in animals, is spread wherever an infected one coughs or sneezes. Wild animals can carry rabies and distemper. Dr. Sequist recommends that people do not keep wild animals as pets.

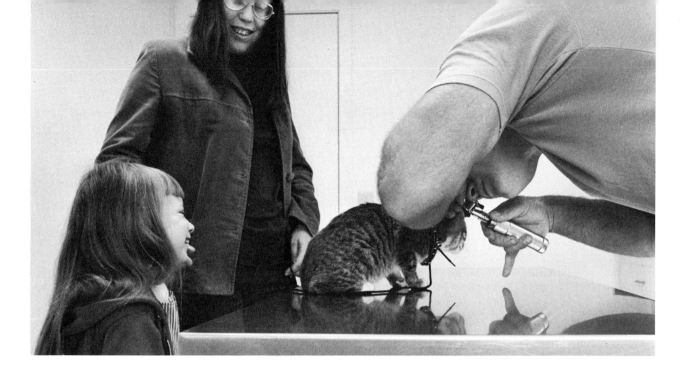

Before Tinkerbell leaves, Dr. Sequist examines her ears for ear mites, which are tiny parasites that can itch and cause infections. He does this examination on all dogs and cats, and the instrument he uses is an *otoscope*. By changing the lens he can make it into an *ophthalmoscope* for checking eyes. Along with a stethoscope, an otoscope-ophthalmoscope is a veterinarian's most important instrument, and a good one can cost over one hundred fifty dollars.

Tinkerbell's ears are clean. She shouldn't have to see the doctor for another year, and that suits Jennifer fine.

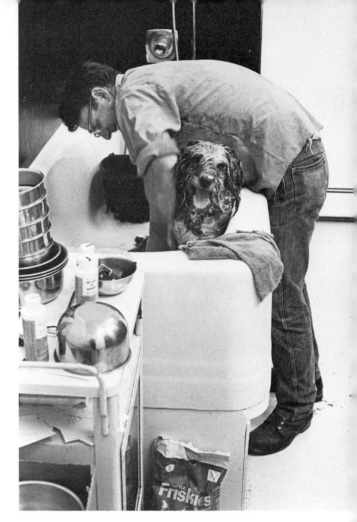

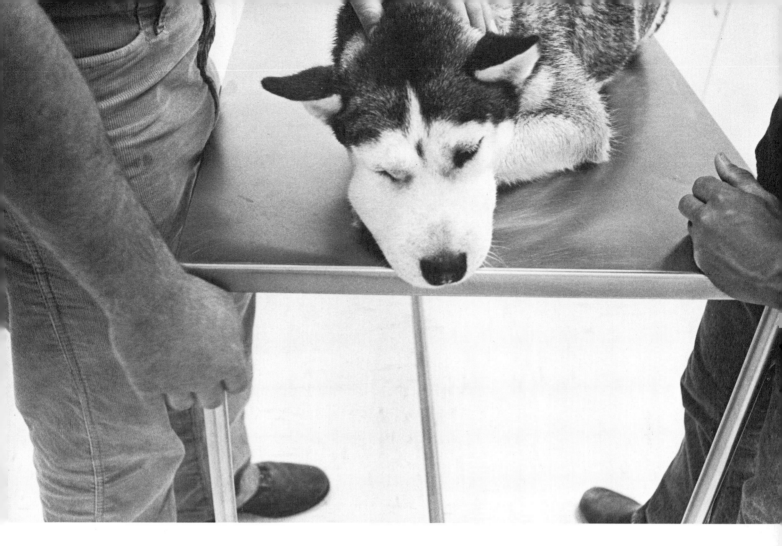

While Dr. Sequist sees patients, Alan Morton does some chores. Alan grew up in England during World War II and worked for veterinarians in Canada before coming to the United States. To Dr. Sequist he's indispensable. He gives shots and helps in surgery and generally serves as nurse, X-ray technician, and handyman, both at the hospital and on the road. He says he doesn't mind walking or bathing dogs, and he likes feeding the Sequist calves, but he doesn't like cutting out hair mats. "If people took care of their dogs and brushed them often," he says, "the dogs wouldn't get hair mats." Dr. Sequist agrees.

The doctor's next patient is a Siberian husky named Puki, who fought a porcupine this morning.

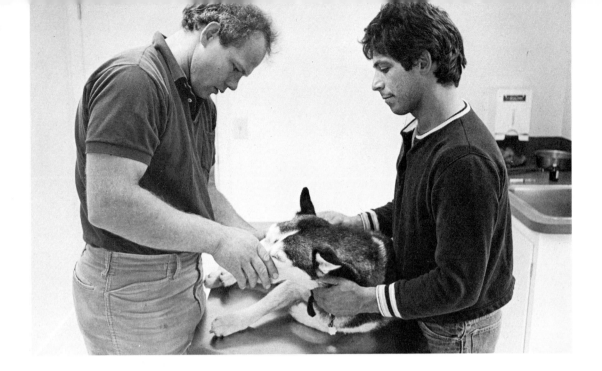

Puki lost, of course. The sharp-quilled porcupine always wins. Puki's owner, Mr. Altomare, thinks that he got all the quills out of Puki's mouth, but Dr. Sequist feels the dog's muzzle all over to be sure.

To examine a patient by touch like this is to *palpate* him, and once again the veterinarian needs a skilled pair of hands. Dr. Sequist can't find any more quills, but he is concerned about the swelling on Puki's face. He thinks that Puki has had an allergic reaction to the quills or to something that was on the quills, such as dust or pollen. Puki needs a shot of a medicine called a *corti-costeroid* to make the swelling go away, and a shot of antibiotic to kill whatever germs were on the quills.

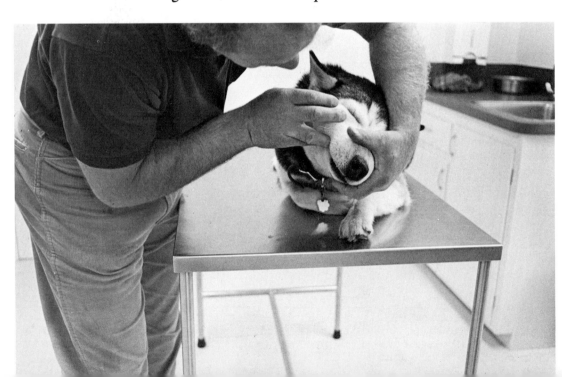

In states like Vermont where porcupines are plentiful, veterinarians are always pulling quills out of dogs. Dr. Sequist says you have to find every one because they can move deeper into a dog's body and cause problems. Quills hurt. They're hollow and sharp and have barbs on the end, so sometimes the doctor needs a knife to cut them out. Contrary to stories, porcupines don't throw their quills, they just let them rub off on attackers.

This is Puki's third visit to the veterinarian to have quills pulled, and it probably won't be her last. Dogs who have been injured by porcupines often attack them again because the dogs want to get back at the thing that hurt them. The only advice that the doctor can give is to keep Puki penned.

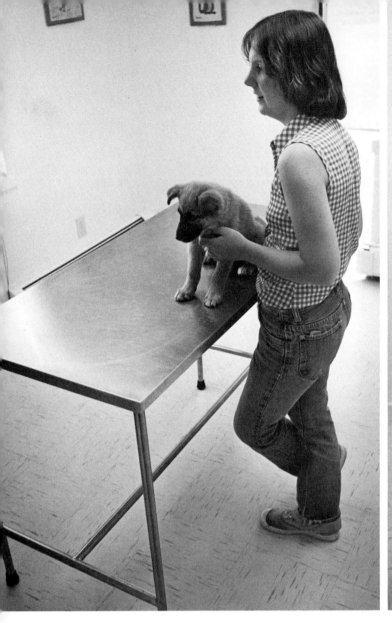

Ten o'clock, and the patients keep coming. A young woman, Miss Case, is worried about Spring, her two-month-old puppy. Spring keeps eating fast and throwing up her food, and she isn't growing as she should. Otherwise, she looks and acts healthy. Is she sick? Can Dr. Sequist help her?

Spring can't say what's wrong with her, of course, so this is an instance where a veterinarian has to be a good detective. When faced with a mysterious case like Spring's, Dr. Sequist always takes the patient's temperature first. Spring's is 102 de-

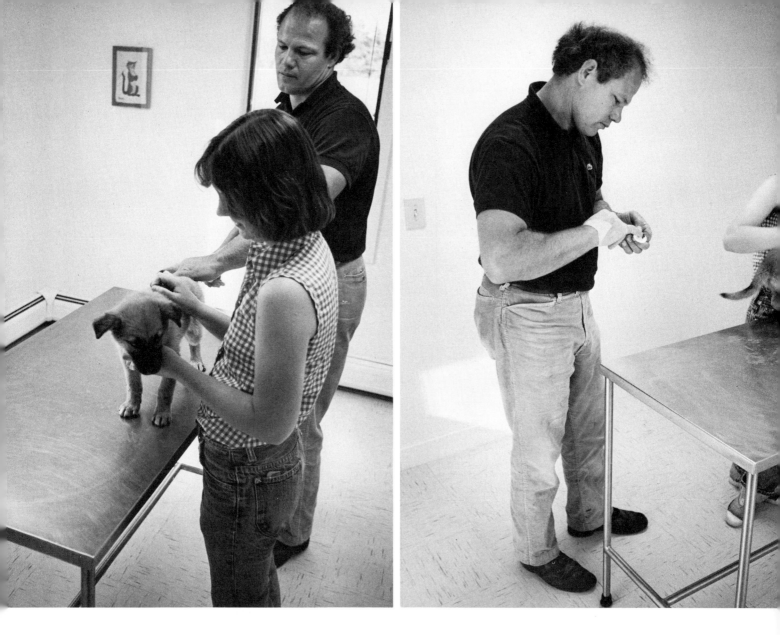

grees Fahrenheit, which is normal for dogs, so the doctor knows she doesn't have a fever. Next he palpates her sides, feeling for strange lumps and bumps.

There are none. Spring's sides, her mouth, and her teeth are all fine. The doctor decides to do a test called a *fecal exam* to see whether Spring has worms. He puts on a rubber glove and collects a sample of Spring's stool, which he puts in a special plastic cup.

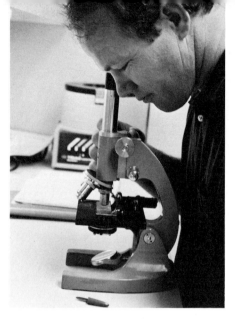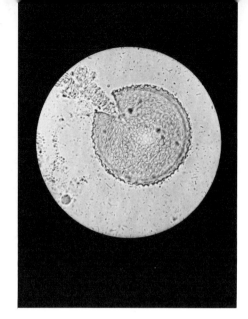

After pouring liquid into the cup, the doctor stirs the mixture with a wooden stick and sets it aside for ten minutes. Worm eggs are tiny. They can only be seen under the microscope. If Spring does have worms, the eggs will rise to the surface of the liquid and attach themselves to the microscope slide that the doctor puts on top.

Ten minutes later, the doctor studies the slide. Of all the many things he does, Dr. Sequist enjoys looking through the microscope just about the most. He says it's like entering a whole different world.

And he finds something! Worm eggs — ascarid worm eggs. So that's why Spring isn't growing. She has worms! Ascarid eggs like this one hatch in a puppy's stomach, and the worms, which are parasites, feed off the puppy's food. The puppy loses weight. If left alone, ascarids can grow to the length of earthworms and make an animal very sick. Spring must have eaten manure, because that is where ascarids breed. Now the doctor knows what to do.

He makes a prescription for Spring. "Give her two pills a day," he tells Miss Case, "and start feeding her cottage cheese with her regular meals. The pills will kill the ascarids, and cottage cheese has protein, which puppies need for growth."

"And can I make her stop gulping and throwing up her food?" asks Miss Case.

"Yes," says the doctor. "Put rocks in her bowl that are big enough so that she'll have to push them aside to get at her food. That will make her eat slower, and the throwing up should stop."

"Thank you," says Miss Case.

Dr. Sequist believes that good nutrition is just as important for animals as it is for people. Often animals get sick because they don't eat the right foods. Once, for example, someone brought his pet goat to the hospital because her hair was falling out, and the doctor discovered that she wasn't getting the right vitamins. So he drew up a list of foods she should eat and gave her some vitamin shots. After a few weeks the problem went away.

Today someone has brought in a stray cat that is so weak from hunger that it can't eat anything by itself. Dr. Sequist has to force-feed it, using a stomach tube.

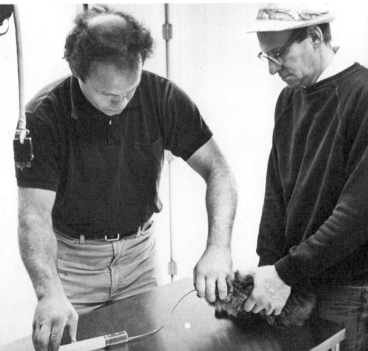

Then he checks out the last of this morning's clinic patients, two Lhasa apsos and a poodle that needed their toenails trimmed.

Afterwards he takes ten minutes to order some drugs from his veterinary supply salesman, Mike Murphy. And then it's eleven o'clock. Time for this morning's surgery.

The patient this morning is a young black Labrador named Tara who has a lump on her leg called a *tumor*. Tumors are caused by many things, but Tara's started last summer when her leg was bumped by a car. If you don't operate on tumors and cut them out early, they can get bigger and bigger and break open and get infected. So Tara's must be removed.

Dr. Sequist is always gentle with surgery patients because he senses their nervousness at times like these.

First the patient must be made to fall asleep. This is done by giving her a shot of anesthetic. For dogs it doesn't take much — just a few c.c.'s.

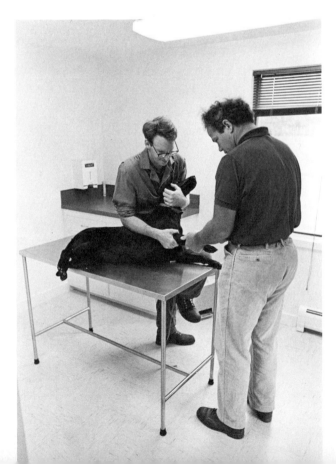

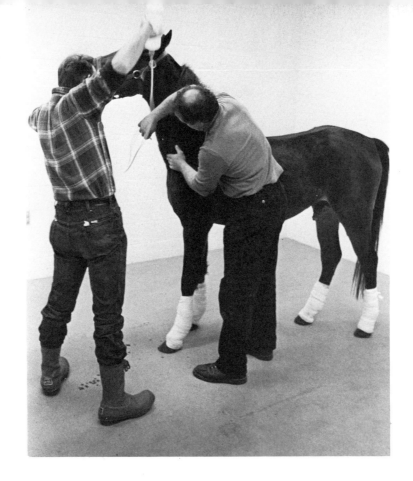

If Tara was bigger, though, she'd get a whole bottle of anesthetic to make her sleepy. And then the operation would be taking place in the big-animal room, where the big patients fall asleep on a floor that's made of rubber.

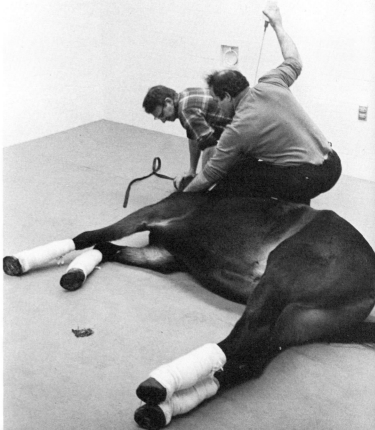

But now the few c.c.'s of anesthetic have taken effect. Tara is fast asleep. Alan moves her quickly to the operating room.

There the doctor puts a tube in her mouth and attaches it to a tank that pumps oxygen and halothane gas into her lungs. The oxygen keeps the patient alive and breathing during the operation, and the halothane keeps her asleep the whole time so she never feels any pain. Halothane is the same kind of gas that dentists use when they pull teeth, and that surgeons use when they operate on people.

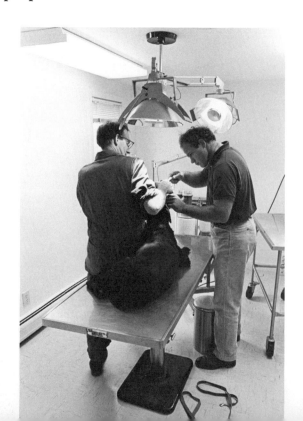

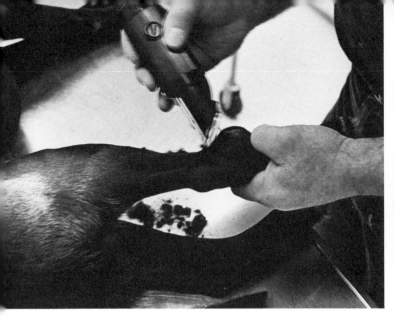
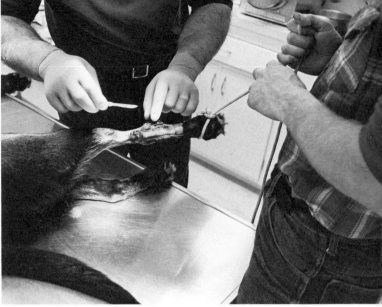

The area around the tumor must be shaved and scrubbed. Alan vacuums the shaved hair away with a vacuum cleaner.

Then with Alan holding the leg steady, the surgery begins. Dr. Sequist says that whenever he performs surgery, he only thinks of the job he must do — he knows he will not hurt the patient. His only concern for Tara now is that she is sleeping comfortably.

Surgery means cleanliness. Before he operates, the doctor always washes his hands with disinfectant and then puts on rubber surgical gloves. Everything that touches the open cut must be sterile, so before each operation the scalpels, the clamps, the forceps, and the scissors are all sterilized in a special machine called an *autoclave*.

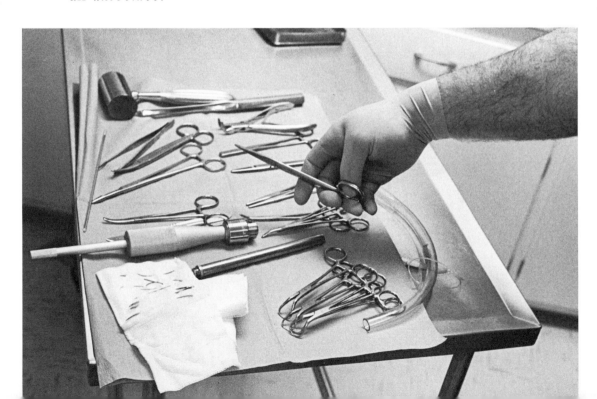

Slowly the tumor is cut away. The doctor always pays attention when he operates so he won't make mistakes.

Finally, thirty minutes after the operation began, the tumor is removed. "It's big," says Dr. Sequist.

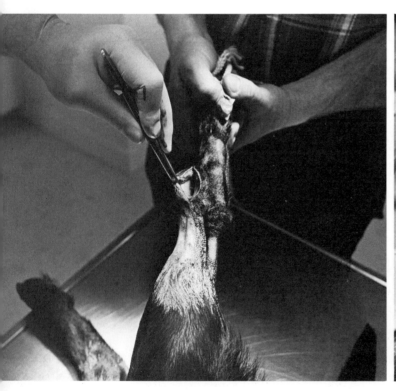 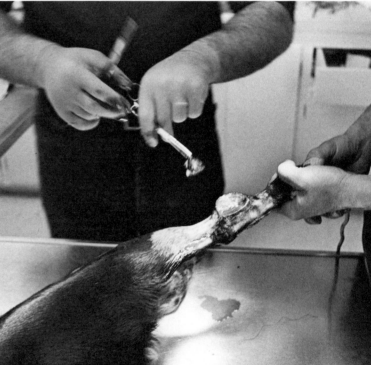

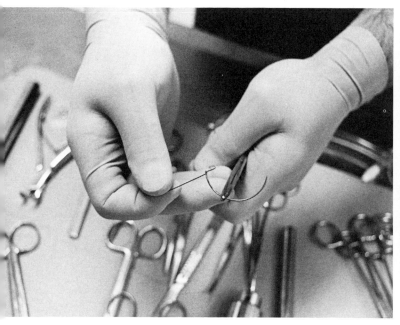 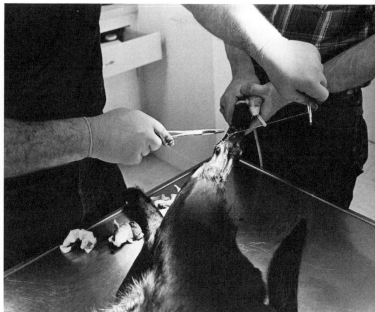

Now the cut must be stitched. The medical word for a stitch is a *suture*, and Dr. Sequist uses a curved surgical needle and black surgical thread to make each one.

Tara doesn't feel anything because she's still fast asleep. Her cut needs twelve sutures, which must stay in for two weeks.

Then the sutured cut must be sprayed with yellow disinfectant to kill any germs that might have gotten on it, and bandaged with a soft elastic tape.

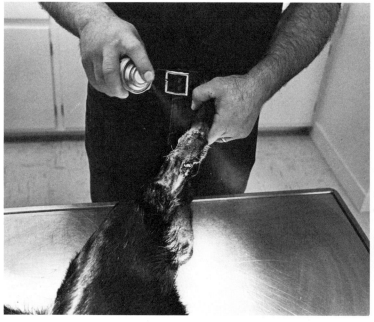 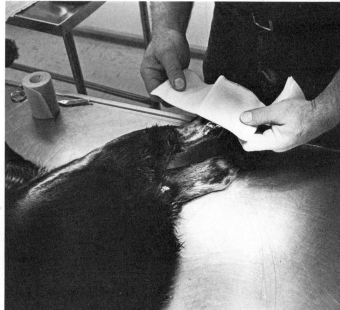

Dr. Sequist is pleased with a job well done. Tara's tumor is gone.

He lifts her onto a wheeled cart called a *gurney* and takes her back to her cage, where she will rest until her master comes for her tomorrow.

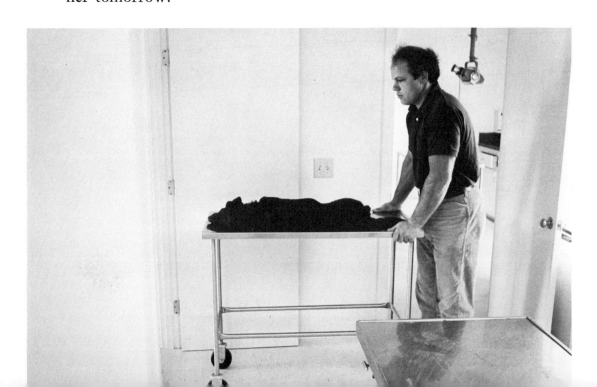

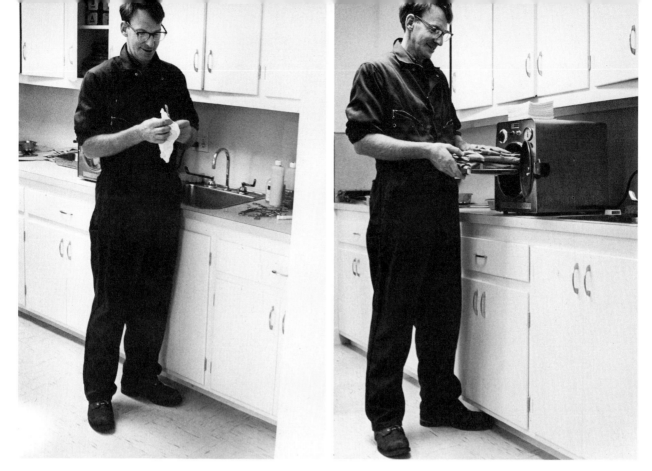

After an operation Alan always washes the instruments and puts them back in the autoclave to be sterilized. And the doctor never leaves the operating room until everything has been cleaned and put away.

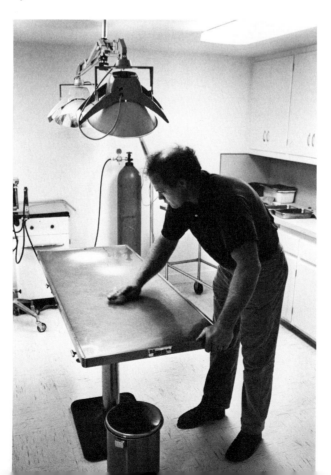

Twelve o'clock. But there's no time for lunch yet. The horse
that was scheduled for X rays has arrived and is waiting for the
doctor in the big-animal room.

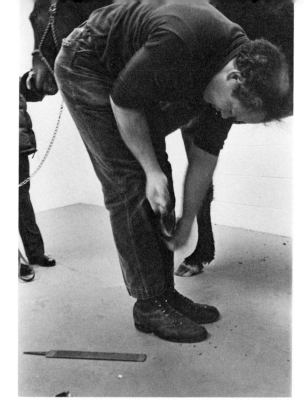

The horse's name is Jamie, and she's twelve years old. A girl named Wendy wants to buy her, so her legs must be X-rayed to see if they are strong.

First Alan wipes Jamie's feet, and then the doctor trims Jamie's hooves so they'll fit flat on the X-ray plate. Dr. Sequist, like every other student, learned hoof-trimming and horse-shoeing in veterinary school.

Dr. Sequist says that the hardest part of X-raying a horse is making her stand still on the metal X-ray plate. Luckily, Jamie is a good horse and doesn't move a muscle. When the right time comes, the doctor asks everyone to leave the room, and then he and Alan take the picture alone. You have to wear special clothing when you X-ray because X-ray waves can hurt you if you're exposed to them long enough.

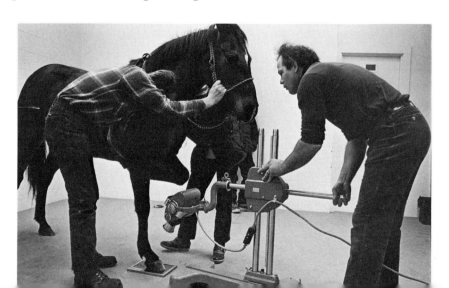

Now Wendy must wait while the doctor develops the X rays.
Ten minutes pass.

The doctor studies the X rays on the viewer.

And they're negative, which means there are no problems. Wendy can buy the horse. Jamie is hers!

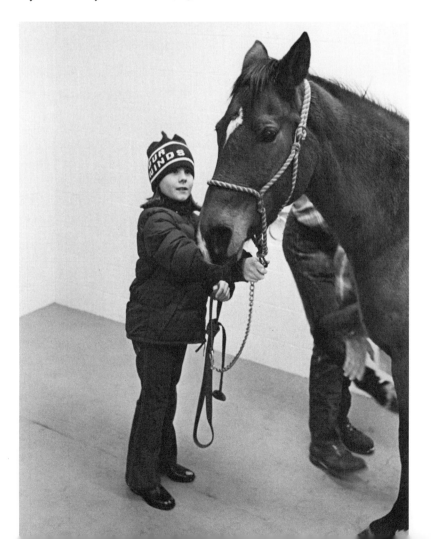

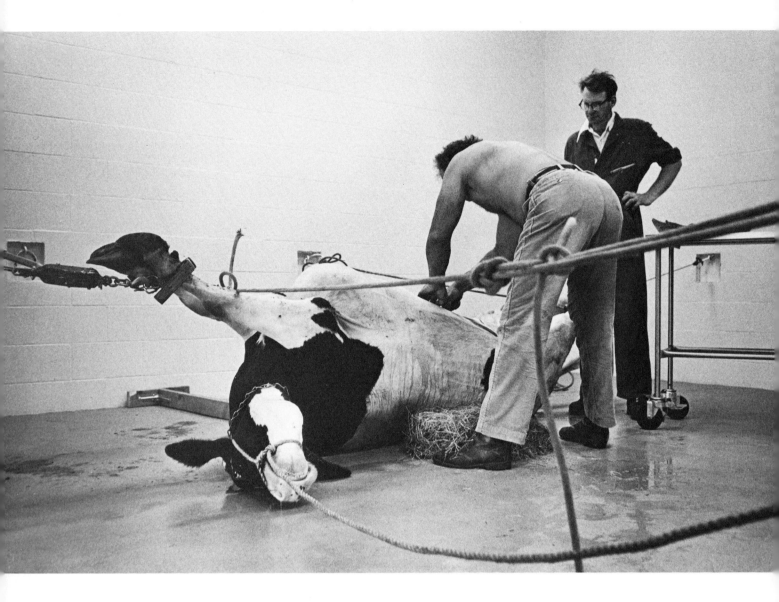

The big-animal room has many uses, but mostly it's used for surgery. Often the doctor operates on cows for a stomach problem called a *displaced abomasum*. Cows have four stomachs, and the fourth, the abomasum, sometimes slips out of place. So the doctor sutures it back where it belongs. The patient is awake the

whole time because the doctor puts only her stomach to sleep with a drug called a *local anesthetic*.

Cows are always shaky after the operation, but usually they can go home and start giving milk again the next day.

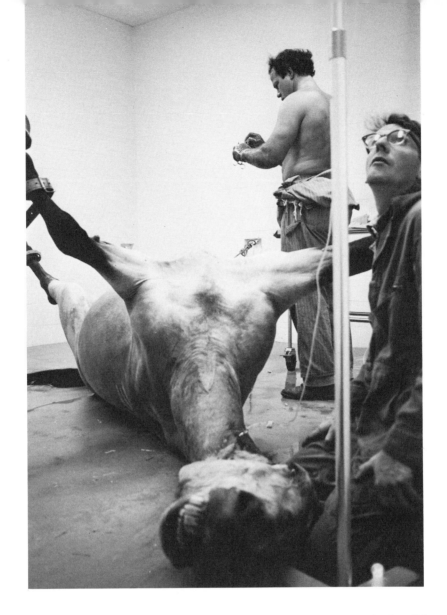

Dr. Sequist also operates on horses. He once saved the life of a horse whose large intestine was twisted. He fixed the twist, and the horse could eat again the next day. Otherwise her intestine would have filled with gas, and she would have died.

Sometimes the doctor allows visitors, such as the local 4-H club, to observe him when he operates.

But now the X rays are done and the big-animal room is quiet. Dr. Sequist and Alan can eat their lunch in peace.

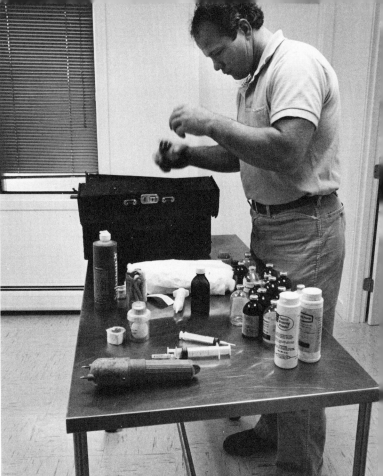

Only part of a veterinarian's day is spent in the hospital. The other part is spent on the road, visiting different stables and farms. After lunch Alan begins packing the car for the long afternoon of travel ahead. Everything the doctor might need to treat an animal is packed in its place in the back seat or in the trunk. Altogether the car carries one thousand pounds of veterinary equipment.

Dr. Sequist takes a moment to clean and refill his kit bag. And then it's one-thirty. The doctor and Alan drive off to this afternoon's calls.

Working with cows can get messy, so the doctor and Alan always wear coveralls and rubber boots when they go into barns.

They enter through the milk house, which is the cleanest part of any barn. It's where the milk tank sits and the milking equipment is stored.

The cows are waiting. Each cow is tied in her own place to a special bar called a *stanchion*.

The calves that need dehorning are taken care of first.

Often a farmer wants to sell a cow, but first, by state law, the cow's blood must be tested for a disease of the reproductive system called *brucellosis*. Since only veterinarians are allowed to take the blood samples, Dr. Sequist finds himself busy nearly every day drawing blood from cows. He draws the sample from a vein on the underside of the cow's tail. Later he delivers the blood to a state laboratory, which makes the test. If a cow does have brucellosis, it's against the law for a farmer to use its milk or to sell the cow for meat.

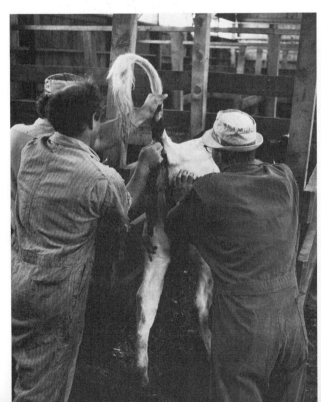

The papers that go with the blood tests must be carefully filled out in threes. Sometimes the paperwork can be a nuisance, especially when the doctor has other work, but it must be done.

Today a farmer, Mr. Sweet, has called because the milk from one of his cows didn't look right this morning. Is the cow sick? The doctor takes a sample of milk from each of the cow's four teats to find out. Dr. Sequist remembers being able to milk cows by hand when he was a teenager. Most farmers milk their cows by machine now.

Normally cows' milk is smooth, white, and creamy, but this milk is full of white flakes. The doctor knows what they mean — the cow has *mastitis*.

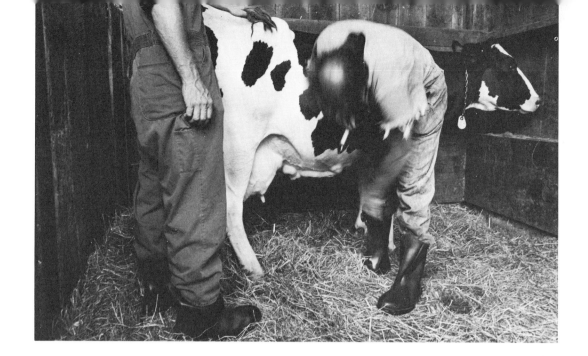

Mastitis is a painful swelling of the milk glands, which is usually caused when bacteria that are on the milking machines get inside a cow's udder. It's very common in dairy cows — and very harmful. If not treated quickly, some kinds of mastitis can spread to other parts of a cow's body and kill her.

Fortunately, Mr. Sweet's Holstein is not very sick, and the shot of penicillin that Dr. Sequist gives her should kill the bacteria and make her well again.

After the doctor has treated the sick cow, he and Alan hose off their boots and wash their hands in the milk house. The milking equipment hangs on the walls. Farmers milk their cows twice a day — once in the morning and once in the afternoon, and Mr. Sweet's milking day often starts as early as five A.M.

One of the most pleasant parts of being a large-animal veterinarian is getting to talk with the farmers. Mr. Sweet and Dr. Sequist talk about everything — from the cost of hay to the size of the last fish they each caught. Today Mr. Sweet introduces the doctor to his grandson, Matt, who is here from Minnesota to help his grandfather on the farm.

After finishing at a farm, the doctor always makes a record of the visit in a kind of diary called a *day book*, and then he calls Sue on the car radio to tell her where he is.

"Nine-nine-six, come in please!"

"Yes?" says Sue.

"Any messages?"

"Only one: Mr. Abair just called and his Jersey cow, Half-Pint, is sick with milk fever. She won't get up. Can you go to see her right away?"

"I'm on my way!" says Dr. Sequist. And he drives off fast.

Milk fever happens when the level of calcium in a cow's blood goes down. This "blood calcium" is a mineral which helps a cow's muscles work. Often when a cow gives birth, her body uses up much of her blood's supply of calcium to make milk for her new baby. Then the cow's muscles get so weak that she falls down and can't move. If she isn't given more calcium fast, she will die.

Dr. Sequist arrives at the Abair place in ten minutes, and Chip Abair takes him right to the patient. Sure enough, Half-Pint is showing all the signs of milk fever. Her head is twisted sideways and her eyes are dull. Her nose is dry and her legs feel cool to the touch. Chip says that she calved two nights ago and that she came down sick this morning. Dr. Sequist is here just in time.

49

While Chip holds the calcium bottle, the doctor puts a needle in the jugular vein in Half-Pint's neck and attaches the needle to the rubber hose. For the next ten minutes the calcium trickles in. You mustn't let it flow in too fast, Dr. Sequist tells Chip, because a lot of calcium rushing through a cow's heart all at once can cause the heart to stop.

The good thing about calcium is that it works fast. By the time the bottle is empty, Half-Pint is feeling her old self again. Dr. Sequist lets her rest for a few minutes.

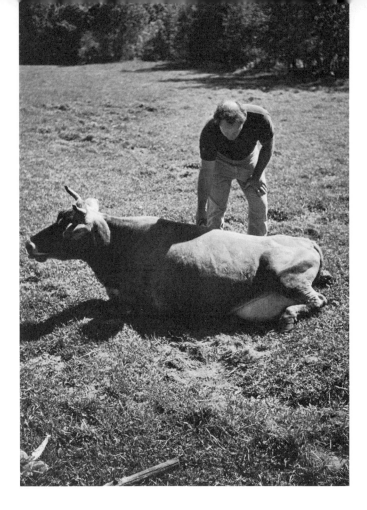

But then she really must get up because it isn't good for a cow's blood circulation for her to stay down so long. So Dr. Sequist pokes her with a battery-operated buzzer prod. The prod gives animals a little shock, and cows don't like the buzzing sound.

Cows rise hind legs first, and horses rise front legs first. Cows are so heavy that Dr. Sequist often wonders how they can stand at all.

Half-Pint is up now, and her milk fever is cured. Tonight she'll be able to see her baby, who has been waiting for her under the trees.

"Was it a bull or a heifer?" asks Dr. Sequist.

"A bull," says Chip. "His name is Teddy."

"Call me if Half-Pint gets sick again," says the doctor.

"Thanks," says Chip. "I will."

For the next hour the doctor visits more farms. Cows are always getting sick, and farmers want them treated quickly so that they don't stop making milk.

At one farm a cow isn't eating, and the farmer thinks that she might have swallowed something metal, such as a nail or a piece of wire. But Dr. Sequist can't hear any signs of "hardware" with his stethoscope, so Alan loads a special instrument for giving pills called a *balling gun* with four big boluses containing B-vitamins and amino acids, which will help bring back the cow's appetite.

It would be easier if a cow would swallow a whole bolus by herself, but she won't, so the balling gun is used to slide the bolus to the back of her throat. Even then, some cows spit the boluses out.

At the next farm, where the doctor has to examine some goats, a baby Holstein just five minutes old is trying to stand. Calves are born all year round but mostly in the spring and the fall.

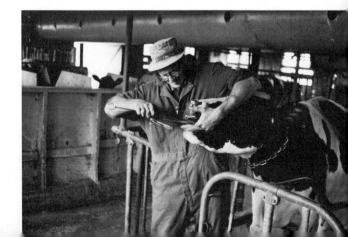

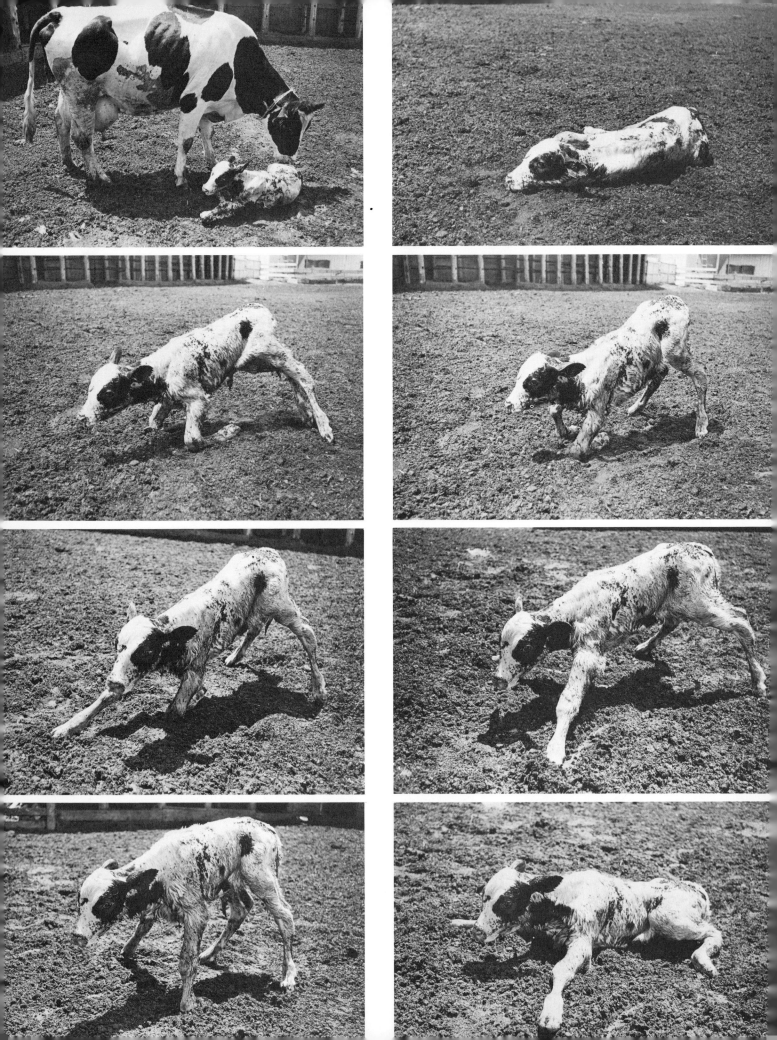

It's now four o'clock. And at the next farm Dr. Sequist visits, something sad happens. A cow that has been down for the past two days won't get up even when the doctor pokes her with the buzzer prod. Often cows just need a little boost, so the doctor and Alan try raising this one with a pair of hip lifters, but they don't work either—the cow just sinks back to the ground. And then the doctor discovers that her hind legs don't work . . . in fact, her whole back end is paralyzed. Why?

The doctor thinks that a heel fly larva has burrowed into the cow's spinal cord. Heel flies are parasites that lay their sticky eggs on cows' legs. The eggs hatch into larvae, which burrow inside the cow's body and then grow into bigger larvae like this one on the cow's back. Later they fall on the ground and turn into new heel flies. The bumps on this cow's back are heel fly larvae waiting to get bigger and fall out, says Dr. Sequist. One of them has somehow gotten into the cow's spinal cord and squeezed off the nerves that control the cow's legs. The cow can't move. The doctor can't help her, and her problems are only going to get worse.

55

So she must die. Tonight after chores the farmer will shoot her with a pistol.

Having to kill an animal is the hardest part of any veterinarian's job, says Dr. Sequist. A good veterinarian does everything he can to save an animal. But if there is nothing he can do, he also knows when an animal should be destroyed rather than allowed to suffer. "You never like having to kill an animal," says the doctor, "but there are times when it must be done."

For the rest of the afternoon the doctor does only easy calls. At one house he docks a lamb's tail, because otherwise the tail will just get dirty and attract flies.

It's always best to dock lambs' tails when the lambs are little because they don't feel as much pain. Afterwards, though, Alan always likes to give them a little comforting.

At another house the doctor deworms a horse. Horses get worms just as dogs and cats do, and the best way to kill the worms is by pumping a special worm-killing medicine into the horse's stomach. Dr. Sequist starts by measuring the medicine into a stainless steel cup.

Then he slides a long plastic tube up the horse's nose and down into its stomach. He has to use the tube because the worm medicine tastes awful and the horse would never drink it himself. The doctor blows air through the tube to help it slide in easier.

He knows when the tube has reached the stomach because he can smell the grass that's there. It smells sweet. Then the doctor pumps in the medicine with a hand pump. Usually horses are a little nervous when the deworming begins, and Dr. Sequist can't blame them. "I'd hate to have a tube put up *my* nose!" he says. But the horses always seem to calm down soon.

He finishes the deworming by blowing in the last of the medicine and sliding out the tube, which he washes immediately afterwards. Most horses get dewormed twice a year, in the spring and in the fall, and because of all the dewormings, these are a veterinarian's two busiest seasons.

One problem that veterinarians see all year round in horses is lameness. Horses can go lame for many reasons; one reason is that some of them can't carry all their weight on their hooves. Dr. Sequist does different things for each lameness depending on how bad it is. He might prescribe pain pills, or give a shot, and sometimes he recommends surgery.

Now the doctor stops at the Carpenter place, where Julie Carpenter's horse, Moccasin, bumped his leg yesterday. Dr. Sequist says that he just needs a little rest.

Sometimes a horse won't eat because his teeth are rubbing into his cheeks or his tongue. Then the teeth have to be filed with a special tool called a *float*.

Five o'clock. Now Dr. Sequist drops Alan off with some blood samples at the University of Vermont's animal pathology lab. That's where the tests are done on the blood that Dr. Sequist takes from different animals. Dr. Kunkel, who is the associate pathologist, checks the blood in. Later the lab technicians will test the blood for different diseases and send a report back to Dr. Sequist's hospital.

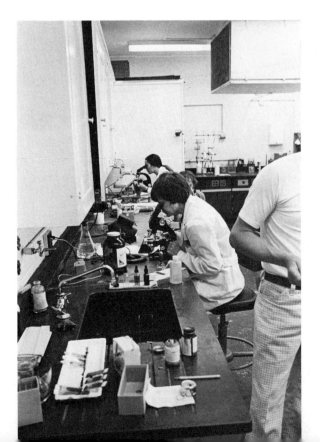

Meanwhile, Dr. Sequist drives to his last patient for the afternoon, a Black Angus bull named Sam.

Sam weighs two thousand one hundred pounds, and his owner, Mr. Steele Griswold, thinks that he has hurt his left hind foot. The question is, how is Dr. Sequist going to handle such a big patient?

Luckily, Mr. Griswold has a special table that tilts and that is built to hold large animals. The men lead Sam into the pen where the table sits, and Dr. Sequist puts the table's straps around Sam's middle. Then he and Mr. Griswold turn the wheels, and slowly and gently Sam is lifted off the ground.

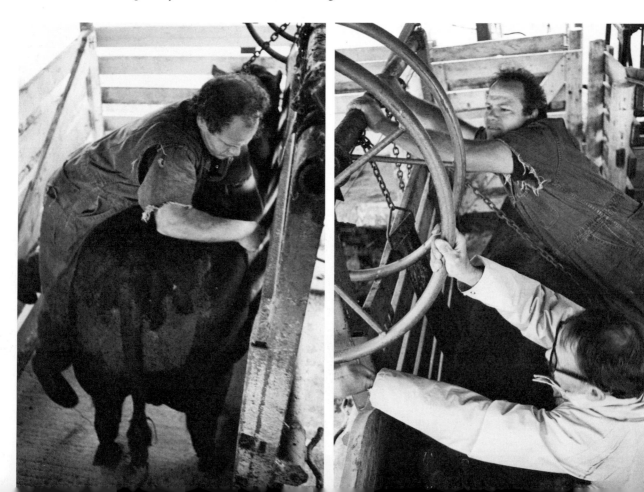

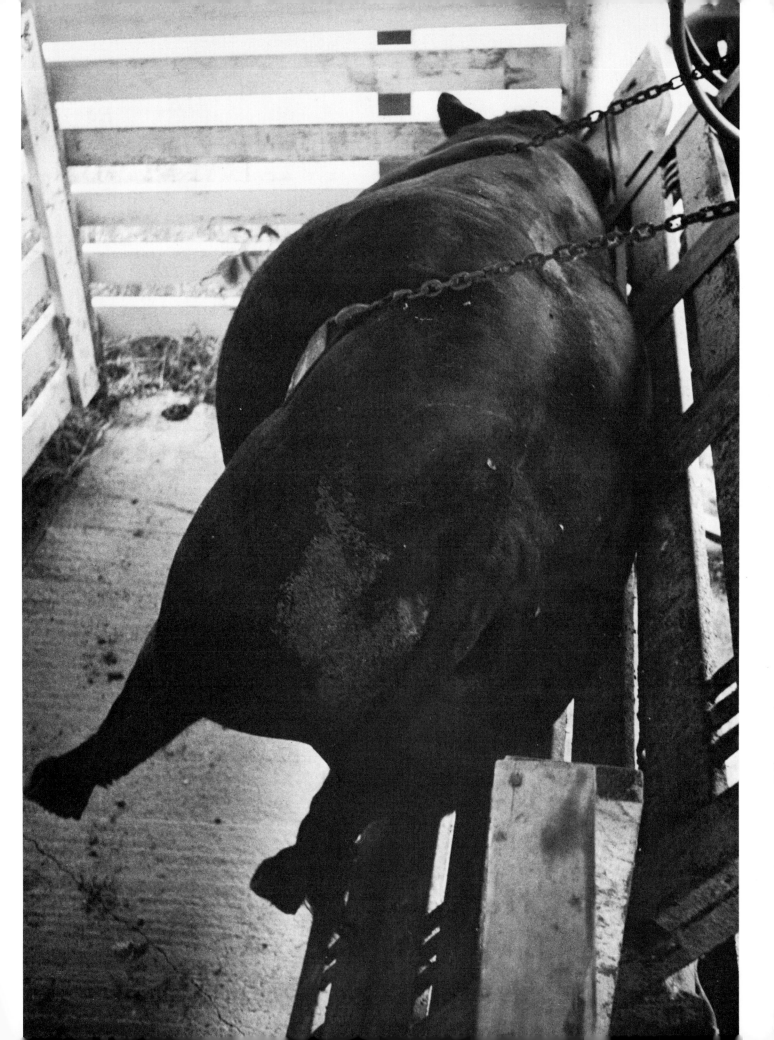

Now it is easy for Dr. Sequist to see the problem. Sam has an infection called an *abscess* on the inside of his hoof. He must have stepped on something sharp, which cut the hoof and started the infection. Hoof abscesses in cattle are something a veterinarian sees nearly every day. Dr. Sequist opens the abscess to let it drain, then wraps Sam's hoof with cotton gauze and adhesive tape, which must stay on for four days.

Throughout the whole procedure, Sam lies quietly on the table. He's Mr. Griswold's favorite bull.

When the bandaging is done the men lower Sam to the ground, and then Mr. Griswold leads him back to his own big pasture. It is six o'clock. The afternoon's calls are done.

After a long afternoon like today's, Dr. Sequist usually likes to stop somewhere for a little snack. Now he picks Alan up at the blood lab, and the two of them stop at a general store.

And then it happens: an emergency. The doctor and Alan are sitting in the car and drinking their sodas when Sue's voice comes over the radio. "Nine-nine-six, car one, come in please."

"Yes," says Dr. Sequist.

"Doctor," says Sue, "the Van Swearingens just called, and their puppy, Star, has been hit by a truck. They don't know how bad he's hurt. They're pretty upset. Shall I tell them you're — "

"Tell them to bring the dog in right away," says Dr. Sequist. "Tell them I'll be back at the hospital in twenty minutes."

"All right," says Sue.

The doctor and Alan toss their empty soda bottles on the car floor, and off they speed to the hospital.

Emergencies can happen any time in the course of a veterinarian's day. Sometimes Dr. Sequist is awakened in the middle of the night by a call to come and take care of a sick or an injured animal. Then he has to get out of bed and go to the emergency even if he is tired or the weather is bad. On nights when there is more than one emergency he gets very little sleep. But he goes . . . because it is his job to go, and because he loves animals so much

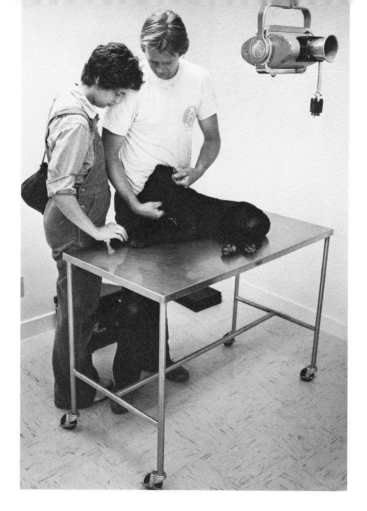

The Van Swearingens and their puppy, Star, are waiting when the doctor arrives twenty minutes later. He rushes in and washes his hands and goes quickly to work.

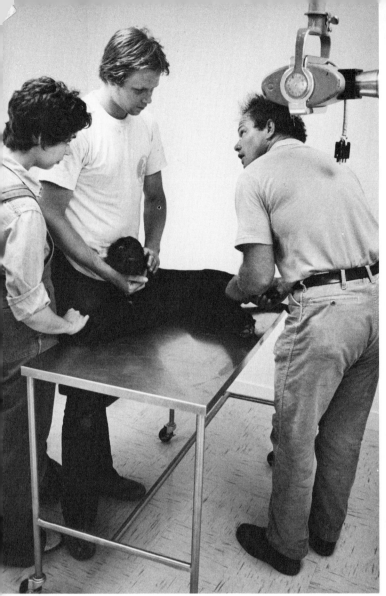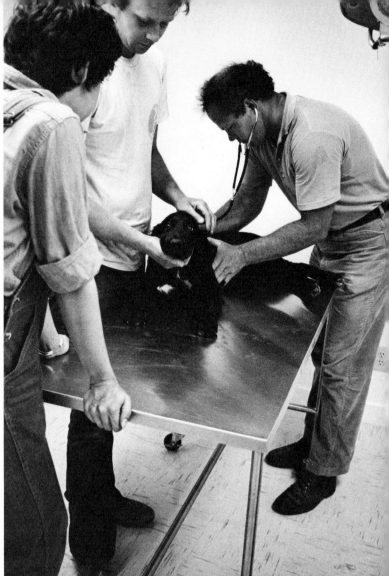

First he palpates Star's legs to check for broken bones, and then he asks the Van Swearingens to explain what happened. Mr. Van Swearingen says that he started the family truck, not noticing that Star was sleeping near the wheels. He knows he hit the dog because he heard a yelp when the truck rolled forward. But he's not sure which part of the body he hit, and he doesn't know how hard.

Dr. Sequist can feel no broken bones but that doesn't necessarily mean that Star is okay. There might be bleeding inside, in which case Star would need an emergency operation. Dr. Sequist listens with his stethoscope for unusual sounds.

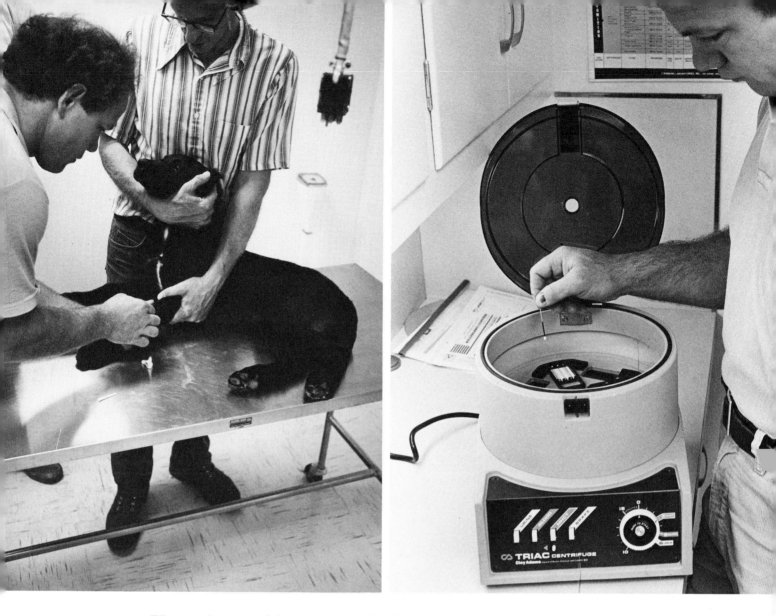

He can hear nothing strange. But he wants to be *sure* that the dog is not bleeding inside, so he decides to do a very special blood test. He draws a sample of blood from Star's paw into a thin glass tube called a *pipette*. And this he puts into a machine called a *centrifuge*, which will separate the blood into its different parts by spinning it around very fast. Ten minutes later he does the test again to compare results.

If Star *is* bleeding inside, the two samples will look different . . . the level of red blood cells in the second sample will be lower than in the first. But if Star *isn't* bleeding inside, the two samples will look the same. Everybody hopes that the samples look the same so that Star won't need an operation.

And then comes the scary moment. Dr. Sequist opens the centrifuge lid and holds the two pipettes up to the light. Both samples look the same after all that spinning. So Star *isn't* bleeding inside! He doesn't need an operation! The Van Swearingens cheer.

As soon as the tests are over, Star is allowed to walk around. He looks as if he's going to be a little stiff for a few days where the truck bumped him, but otherwise he's fine. The Van Swearingens are quite relieved. They thank Dr. Sequist and write him a check for the cost of the visit, and then they thank him again.

Eight o'clock. Now Alan walks the last of the animals for the night, and Dr. Sequist goes to the cage room to see how his surgery patient is doing. Tara is coming along fine from her tumor operation this morning. She will be able to go home with her family early tomorrow.

And then there is nothing more to do. Dr. Sequist turns the FM radio on for the animals in the cage room to make them feel a little less homesick tonight, and then he puts on his coat. It has been a busy day, twelve hours long, but for a veterinarian not an unusual one. The doctor still has phone calls to make to clients after supper, and he never knows if tonight might bring another emergency case like the one he just had with Star. He does know he can expect another busy day tomorrow with more animal patients, more traveling, and more surgery. . . .

But for now the hospital lights are out, and the switchboard is silent. The veterinarian's day is done.

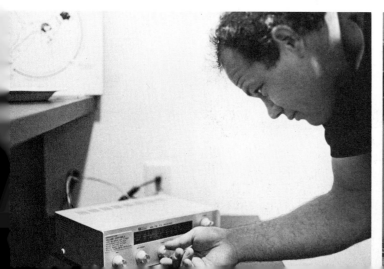

He can go home.

J
636.089
Ja

Jaspersohn, William
A day in the life of a
veterinarian.